VERANDA

A ROOM *of* ONE'S OWN

VERANDA

A ROOM *of* ONE'S OWN

PERSONAL RETREATS & SANCTUARIES

KATHRYN O'SHEA-EVANS

HEARST
books

Introduction

When Virginia Woolf wrote *A Room of One's Own*, her essay on why having your own private quarters fuels free-range thinking, her title of choice was just five little words, yet they were instantly powerful. The expression, "a room of one's own" has endured for nearly 90 years because its sentiment—that you need to carve out your own space to live your best life—rings unequivocally true today, as anyone who's ever shared a crowded space with others will attest. When you create a personal, tailored-to-you bolt-hole, you may find that you're happier and more successful, and that you feel truly at peace. (Fitting, then, that when picturing some of history's most luminous women—Bunny Mellon, Pauline de Rothschild, Fleur Cowles—you may also conjure up their buffed-to-a-high-sheen homes, so essential are they to their identities.)

If you love being at home as much as I do, forging personal spaces all around you is essential. It's a lesson *Veranda* espouses in every issue. The rooms within these pages, all carefully chosen from *Veranda*'s archives, are more than beautiful—they're

evocative of the souls that live there, whether cocooned in toile for Francophile splendor or lacquered at every turn, radiating palpable glamour. The designers behind them often work like anthropologists, sussing out exactly how their clients live so they can help them— with even the most minute fabric choice or layer of paint—improve their daily experience, brandishing art and antiques the way some psychiatrists wield prescriptions.

Gloria Vanderbilt was right when she said, "Decorating is autobiography." I know it, because when I look around my own rooms, I see every decade of my life on display, from the tintypes my husband and I had captured of ourselves one autumn in Lancaster, Pennsylvania, down to an early print of Jules Breton's *La Glaneuse* I picked up in Ireland in college. Wherever your eyes go, *there we are*. I hope you find enough inspiration in this book to take it as a muse—and make every square foot of your home your very own.

DREAMY
bedrooms

It's the height of irony that unruly children are routinely banished to their bedrooms— what better Narnia could there be for young sprites than their toy-stocked quarters? As adults, we must remember to banish ourselves— for it's in this most private of private spaces, the inner sanctum, where we can truly recharge. Create a bedroom that both coddles and restores you, leave your tech gadgets at the door, and watch your days grow longer and more serene.

Cozify the hideaway with all manner of cosseting details, starting with the four walls—perhaps green suede walls with vigor (page 29) or mural-esque wallpaper for a palatial feel (page 39). A canopy atop the bed furnishes decadence befitting Buckingham Palace (page 22); stocking a space with carefully edited antiques transports you to a gentler era (page 38). Whatever you dream up, make your bedroom a fairy tale—as romantic as a bedtime story, for you alone.

CHAPTER OPENER: A headboard made from a vintage suzani helps turn this SoHo aerie by Katie Leede into a sexy, relaxing, and easy retreat. ABOVE: An overscale paisley makes for a fresh and modern master bedroom in this Manhattan pied-à-terre by Cathy Kincaid. OPPOSITE PAGE: In Montecito, California, Richard Hallberg emphasizes a sculptural headboard with symmetrically placed etchings that draw the eye up.

"While I find balance and a rhythm in personal spaces to be important principles, I think varying the textures is what makes it inviting. Smaller, more personal spaces give us a close-up and tactile experience with the objects and materials surrounding us. Mixing a cashmere throw, polished silver frames with family members' photos, a shell or piece of art collected on a trip—these are the tactile layers that make me most happy in intimate spaces."

—Tammy Connor

OPPOSITE PAGE: Tammy Connor adds casual cheer to a pair of iron-frame beds with antique quilts perfectly befitting a 19th-century Tennessee cabin. FOLLOWING PAGES: Designer Tammy Connor maximizes a low attic ceiling by placing rope beds under the eaves, which are lined with curtains for magical privacy.

ABOVE: A wall of antiqued mirrors behind the headboard of this Manhattan home by Jeffrey Bilhuber maximizes the light. OPPOSITE PAGE: Exquisite details, such as Moroccan ceilings and keyhole doors, can transform the usual four walls into otherworldly respites.

ABOVE: A canopy-topped bed fit for royalty provides stately slumber in this Virginia home by Suzanne Kasler. OPPOSITE PAGE: Subtly striped linen fabric in an oatmeal hue softens the antique reproduction four-poster bed in this Tennessee home by Tammy Connor.

FACING PAGE: A flower-petal pendant chandelier adds a playful note to a classic Park Avenue master bedroom by Celerie Kemble.

ABOVE: A custom toile cocoons a four-poster Los Angeles bed by Anthony Baratta in Francophile delight.
OPPOSITE PAGE: Charlotte Moss decked the master bedroom of her summer home in East Hampton, New York in romance, by way of antique French botanical paintings, porcelain flowers, and wallpaper in a delicate floral motif.

ABOVE: Green suede-like wallcovering swaddles the master bedroom of Thomas Hamel's Sydney, Australia home, softening its English Regency bed. OPPOSITE PAGE: Malachite-inspired wallpaper in Andrew Brown's Alabama home creates a jewel-box sleeping space that evokes an old Dorothy Draper maxim: "If it looks right, it is right."

ABOVE: A Nick Olsen–designed getaway in Dutchess County, New York, has a bedroom that's a study in textures—leather, wool, and wood—in varying shades of chocolate. OPPOSITE PAGE: James Carter's Birmingham, Alabama, master bedroom is painted a rich green he calls both strong and cozy; the Regency chair and stool add a welcome dose of antiquity. FOLLOWING PAGES: A blue-and-white palette unifies a bedroom layered with patterns in Suzanne Tucker and Timothy Marks's Montecito bungalow.

ABOVE: A Braquenié tree-of-life pattern enlivens a guest room and contrasts with the headboard's stripe at Mark D. Sikes's Hollywood Hills home. OPPOSITE PAGE: A combination of small-scale prints lends charm to a bedroom in a Dallas penthouse designed by Cathy Kincaid. FOLLOWING PAGES: Lucite and mirrored finishes evoke optical illusions in the Dallas bedroom of Jan Showers, where a custom canopy's parrot-green silk interior yields maximalist drama.

ABOVE: Cathy Kincaid creates a soothing, serene retreat in a Manhattan bedroom, with peach-hued custom fabrics and time-tested antiques. OPPOSITE PAGE: A master bedroom in Manhattan by Miles Redd, layered with varying fabrics united in the color blue, creates a calming envelope that's anything but staid.

ABOVE: Cheryl Skoog Tague installed bookcase cabinets to divide a bedroom from a sitting area in her New York abode, but allowed light to flow through them. OPPOSITE PAGE: Varying fabric choices—suede, linen, and wool among them—create a welcoming cocoon in Shawn Henderson's upstate New York farmhouse.

ABOVE: Decorating a bedroom with walls, curtains, and a headboard in the same fabric—as Cheryl Skoog Tague did in her New York home—turns it into a confection. OPPOSITE PAGE: The beauty is in the details of designer Alidad's London bedroom, where a custom headboard with gold braid trim and a bedcover made from a 19th-century suzani are an antidote to winter drizzle. FOLLOWING PAGES: Curtains and walls in the same fabric bring cohesion to the Manhattan apartment of Peter Dunham.

Nooks of Wonder

Occasionally, stealing away for a quiet moment in the bedroom isn't enough of a reprieve from our technology-addled lives. On those days, only the most clandestine and covert hideaways will do: a Directoire bed tucked under the eaves of a roofline (page 52) or a leather daybed set under a contemplative window view (page 49). You can make previously unused spaces like these utilitarian if you prefer—as Shawn Henderson did with an entry turned mudroom in his upstate New York farmhouse (page 51). But our favorite nooks have nothing to do with function and everything to do with fun—just enough room for you, a frothy cocktail, and an equally frothy book. Do not disturb.

ABOVE: An antique camelback needlepoint sofa turns this Bellport, New York, stairwell landing by Thomas O'Brien and Dan Fink into a destination. OPPOSITE PAGE: Alessandra Branca made this guest room alcove into a toile dream of a reading nook in the Georgetown neighborhood of Washington, D.C.

ABOVE: Next to floor-to-ceiling windows a daybed forms a contemplative retreat within John Saladino's Montecito residence. OPPOSITE PAGE: For her Dallas clients, Cathy Kincaid added a custom striped banquette to a corner, turning it into a charming reading perch.

ABOVE: A foyer becomes a makeshift mudroom, with under-bench baskets for storage, in Shawn Henderson's upstate New York farmhouse. OPPOSITE PAGE: An antique daybed in a room by Kathryn M. Ireland furnishes an intimate dressing nook with a sense of the Old World.

ABOVE LEFT: A Directoire bed converts an eave into a napping nook in architect James Carter's intentionally rambling, quirky Birmingham house, designed with Jane Hawkins Hoke. ABOVE RIGHT: In delicate pink hues, the tiled sitting room of this Dallas home by Emily Summers is a dreamy retreat. OPPOSITE PAGE: An Atlanta dressing room, bathed in pale pinks by designer Melanie Turner, warms up the energetic Sputnik-inspired chandeliers.

studies for the
SOPHISTICATE

Authors Roald Dahl and Virginia Woolf had one thing in common—and it wasn't a protracted list of best sellers. It's that they wrote some of their most adulated work in teensy, tailored-to-them rooms that were truly all their own (Dahl worked in a backyard hut, Woolf in a former toolshed). As Steve Jobs's former garage would testify, sometimes the greatest thinking occurs in the unlikeliest of places—as long as it feels like yours, it can act as muse. When you're assembling your study, adapt it to your own design yearnings, be they deliciously treacly (a Victorian-inspired den; page 92) or grandiose (ornate hand-painted wall-coverings that depict a rousing scene, pages 76–77). Visually extend an intimate space by tricking the eye, perhaps installing Lucite shelves in a small library (page 58), or placing a sectional sofa flush against a wall—anything to expand your margins (page 61).

CHAPTER OPENER: A painting by Susan Vecsey would even entice procrastinators to work in this fabric-walled Manhattan study area by Tammy Connor. ABOVE: Use glass or Lucite shelving against a mirrored wall, as Celerie Kemble did in this Park Avenue home, to make a small study feel vast. OPPOSITE PAGE: A quiet corner can be all you need for a work space, such as this one that features an antique French desk in James Carter's Birmingham home.

"You don't need decoration. You need an exquisite collection of furniture, fabrics, art, lighting, and personal effects."

—Alessandra Branca

OPPOSITE PAGE: High-gloss trim brings crisp detail to this Chicago lounge by Alessandra Branca, where a sectional pushed against one wall maximizes the space.

60

ABOVE: Kelli Ford and Kirsten Fitzgibbons use a sharp geometric fabric as a surprising and worldly backdrop for fine antiques in Dallas. OPPOSITE PAGE: This Fifth Avenue apartment's previous owner, Diana Ross, presides over the study by Jeffrey Bilhuber, where walls lacquered in a rust hue bring it down to earth.

"We named our home Patina Farm for a reason. It's the idea that you use natural materials and let them age gracefully over time—as I'm trying to do myself."

—Brooke Giannetti

ABOVE: Floor-to-ceiling curtains create a striking backdrop in Andrew Brown's Alabama study. OPPOSITE PAGE: Bold wallcovering brings a hint of the outdoors into Thomas O'Brien and Dan Fink's Bellport, New York, home office.

ABOVE: Cathy Kincaid selected a subtly patterned fabric to cover furniture, walls, and windows, creating a cozy library with a bird's-eye view of Manhattan's cityscape. OPPOSITE PAGE: A bold indigo pattern enlivens this tented Dallas den by Emily Summers.

FACING PAGE: With a canopied French daybed, a Manhattan home office designed by Vicente Wolf converts to a guest suite.

FACING PAGE: Floor-to-ceiling columns bring unabashed grandeur to the Litchfield County, Connecticut, library of designer Robert Couturier.

"What's important to me is authenticity, that no material is fake. I would rather have less but have what is original and real."

—Peter Nolden

FACING PAGE: In Peter Nolden's German country cottage, the study's blue cupboard holds a bed, a common farmhouse feature in the 18th century.

76

ABOVE: Art lends an exceptionally studious air, and a slipper chair provides a perch for additional tomes in Thomas O'Brien and Dan Fink's Bellport, New York, library. OPPOSITE PAGE: Cobalt walls provide an unexpected backdrop to a circa 1920 chandelier in this Nick Olsen–designed country home in Dutchess County, New York.

ABOVE: Walls paneled in antique pine bring understated warmth to a Dallas penthouse by Cathy Kincaid. OPPOSITE PAGE: A vintage cane chair and antique Khotan rug furnish Suzanne Tucker and husband Timothy Marks's Montecito home with storied history.

"I love intimate spaces because I'm obsessed with humanism and storytelling. These types of rooms are biographical-fictions . . . a mélange of mirror and dreams where we see ourselves, define ourselves, comfort ourselves, and expand ourselves. I think the good designer is an anthropologist—it requires a certain amount of daring and erudition; to take risks, stimulate the senses, and explore personal style. You can tell the designers who work viscerally— their work is utterly uplifting in its experiential quality which, to me, is entirely the point of design."
—Colette van den Thillart

FACING PAGE: Juxtaposed against a painting by James Lahey, geometric objects top terrazzo garden tables in the Toronto home of Colette van den Thillart.

ABOVE: Nineteenth-century Russian chairs are anything but business as usual in Colette van den Thillart's reading space. OPPOSITE PAGE: Assorted curiosities, such as a bronze rhinoceros from a Paris flea market, create an erudite atmosphere in John Oetgen and John Lineweaver's Atlanta library. FOLLOWING PAGES: Boring Manhattan storage room no longer: Nick Olsen matches a sectional to inky-blue lacquered walls, transforming it into a glamorous den.

ABOVE: Purple accents add richness to rooms in warm neutrals, as in Colette van den Thillart's Toronto sitting room, with a Hans Wegner wing chair. OPPOSITE PAGE: Cheryl Skoog Tague outfitted her study with animalia—a mood lifter—but added linen curtains for softness. FOLLOWING PAGES: Linen walls and striped curtains cozify a Malibu library by Martyn Lawrence Bullard.

Balanced Books

Nothing says so much about a person as their holdings—their literary holdings. The books we select to live with us could very well be considered roommates, for all their personality and plot lines (left). Choose carefully: every spine tells your story and connotes your interests, be it early 20th century Southern female writers lining your fireplace mantel or Edwardian-era novels stashed in teetering stacks at your bedside. There's never shame in a dippy beach read— but if you find yourself hiding them away in a credenza, we won't tell.

ABOVE: Neutral-hued book spines jibe with the furniture upholstery in this Manhattan pied-à-terre by architect and designer Daniel Romualdez. OPPOSITE PAGE: Painted paneling with an aged patina infuses a new California house by architect M. Carbine Restorations, and designed by Laurie Steichen, with a storied feel.

Balanced Books

ABOVE: Eclectic objects and beloved books combine in cinematic fashion in Susan Ferrier's 1920s Atlanta Tudor. OPPOSITE PAGE: A dramatic Tony Duquette chandelier presides over a guest-room-meets-library designed by Hutton Wilkinson in Malibu, California, where adobe walls are painted in a custom red and the Louis XVI–style daybed is dressed in hand-blocked Indian cotton.

ART-OF-LIVING
rooms

It's almost imperative for the sitting room to be the most showstopping chamber in any home—it's certainly the most see-and-be-seen. When guests arrive for cocktail hour, they're often whisked here even before drinks are summoned from the bar—it's a de facto host extraordinaire. So if a living room is lacking in spirit, no matter how much champagne is flowing, it will feel like design drudgery—lifeless and banal. Turn it into a space worthy of its name by making it the place that exudes trademarks of your life, whether that means erecting a paean to energetic glamour in the form of a peach-pink ladies lounge with a red tufted banquette (page 129) or an ode to globe-trotting, chinoiserie stacked up like so many far-flung adventures (page 102). Compact living rooms can appear to expand with a few key designer sleights of hand: monotone color schemes and vertically hung wall objets can inflate ceiling heights (page 103); waiflike bronze furniture lends levity (page 121), and admiral-blue-lacquered walls seduce like the proverbial jewel box (page 118).

CHAPTER OPENER: A Damien Hirst print inspired the kaleidoscopic patterns in this Chicago living room by Alessandra Branca, where the energetic hues make the intimate space feel special. ABOVE: In his neutral-on-neutral living room, Mark D. Sikes replaced windows with French doors for easy access to the garden. OPPOSITE PAGE: Walls painted high-gloss black ground the array of furnishings in Andrew Brown's Alabama home, including Victorian side chairs in silk ikat and an antique bergère.

ABOVE: A Swedish-inspired palette by Jim Howard brightens a Westchester County, New York, home; the 1970s cocktail table was purchased in Paris. OPPOSITE PAGE: An antique chinoiserie panel is a whimsical counterpoint to the formal French limestone floors of a Dallas entryway designed by Cathy Kincaid FOLLOWING PAGES: A custom blue lacquer unifies the kitchen and family room of this Manhattan apartment by designer Tammy Connor and architect John B. Murray. A tilting oculus brings natural light into the adjacent stairwell.

ABOVE: Treasured mementos on Andrew Brown's 18th-century Chinese desk personalize the space.
OPPOSITE PAGE: In the Montecito bungalow of Suzanne Tucker and Timothy Marks, a pair of slipcovered chairs, adjacent to an 18th-century French limestone mantel, set a relaxed mood. FOLLOWING PAGES: Purple accents add richness to rooms in warm neutrals, such as in Collette van den Thillart's Toronto sitting room.

ABOVE: A light palette of cream, white, and pale blues lends a relaxed air to Kathryn M. Ireland's Venice, California, living room. OPPOSITE PAGE: Exposed wood beams and a painted floor serve as a rustic backdrop for exuberantly upholstered furniture in this Dutchess County, New York, sitting area by Nick Olsen.

"I don't want things to match, but I always weave in something familiar that leads you into the next room."

—Ashley Whittaker

OPPOSITE PAGE: A New York townhouse by Ashley Whittaker is a soothing, artful mélange of vivid hues and calming textures, with art by Agnes Barley.

112

FACING PAGE: Designer Nick Olsen lined an Upper East Side sitting area in a luminous metallic shell that amplifies vibrant upholstery.

114

ABOVE: Marston Luce selected relaxed, linen-sheathed seating in the living area of his 15th-century stone farmhouse in Dordogne, France. OPPOSITE PAGE: Luce revitalized a *canapé Régence* with red linen upholstery that anchors the compact seating area.

"I love color relationships more than anything else. If I show you a sample of taxicab-yellow lacquer, you might think it looks like shellacked dried egg yolk. But if you put it with blues and greens, soft grays and reds, it takes it down a notch and gives you the feeling of brandy held up to the firelight."

—Miles Redd

OPPOSITE PAGE: A Louis XV desk and antique chandelier provide sedate balance in this Miles Redd–designed Manhattan living room, with a custom sofa in olive and walls lacquered peacock blue.

ABOVE: A Portuguese needlepoint rug adds pattern and texture to a neutral Long Island living room by Frank de Biasi and architect Leonard Woods; slender furniture lends levity. OPPOSITE PAGE: In a Dallas music room designed by Cathy Kincaid, panels of patterned fabric emit an exotic atmosphere, along with Louis XVI fauteuils.

ABOVE: Classic furnishings and large-scale art enliven the rustic, oak-paneled room of John Oetgen and John Lineweaver, where an oversize photograph by Hugh Hales-Tooke acts as another window. OPPOSITE PAGE: Mirrored accents and glass tables bestow sparkle above a custom banquette in the Dallas townhouse of Jan Showers.

ABOVE: An aesthetic rival for the 18th-century Chinese silk wall panels, archival Bevilacqua velvet upholsters a sofa in Ann and Gordon Getty's 1913 San Francisco residence. OPPOSITE PAGE: A 17th-century Flemish tapestry takes pride of place in Alidad's London apartment, anchoring the custom roll-arm sofa.

"I think as we get older, we all want to live in settings that feel lighter, brighter, and cleaner. I subtract more than I add."

—Carolyn Malone

ABOVE: An exaggerated pelmet in a New Jersey living room designed by Miles Redd disguises the low window by drawing the eye upward. OPPOSITE PAGE: Situated off the entry hall of an Atlanta home by Melanie Turner and architects Pak Heydt & Associates, the ladies' lounge is the epitome of glamour, with a vintage chandelier and high-gloss peach-pink walls. FOLLOWING PAGES: The living room of the same Atlanta home by Turner and Pak Heydt & Associates marries classical influences with contemporary flair—such as a sofa in Scalamandré tiger-striped velvet.

Art with Impact

If you have ever received a piece of art as a gift, feigned delight and undying gratitude, then hurriedly found it a new home on the shelves of a local charity shop, you're in the majority. Art, like jewelry, is a most personal purchase: either it stirs something in your very soul, or it calls to mind the bombastic artifice of the roadside hotel. When you find a piece you love, give it pride of place: set against a halo of light created by an antique mirror (above) or anchoring a seating area (left)—wherever you're apt to land a gaze most. Keep it well lit, and it will speak to you at all hours.

ABOVE LEFT: An unframed antique portrait lends an aura of history to Colette van den Thillart's Canadian lakeside retreat. ABOVE RIGHT: Shawn Henderson painted walls and floor shades of gray to spotlight a raw-edge wood shelf—and its curated assemblage of objets. OPPOSITE PAGE: A painting by Robert Courtright echoes the neutral yet saturated colors of John Saladino's own Montecito home.

ABOVE: A photograph by Massimo Listri with great depth of field visually expands the entry hall of a Manhattan apartment, with architecture by McBride Architects and design by Alecia Stevens. OPPOSITE PAGE: Don't forget the doors: outside a powder room in Alidad's London apartment, a hallway is lined with a faux suede trimmed in gold braid.

EXQUISITE

powder rooms

In real estate parlance, powder rooms get short shrift as "half baths." Yet stylewise, they could never be considered "half" of anything. Often utilized by dinner party guests, powder rooms are an ideal locale for a bit of decorating braggadocio: turn them into a jewel box so pretty it doesn't need jewels by selecting a gutsy, evocative motif and memorable color scheme. Their intrinsically Lilliputian footprints allow for over-the-top decorating choices that might make your head spin in larger doses: stone-blue silk wallpaper (page 143), hand-painted murals (page 151), or glimmering mirrors lining each and every wall and surface (page 147). Dim lighting casts visitors—and yourself, stealing away for a quiet moment—in a luminous glow. Some of the most remarkable powder rooms push the respite envelope, creating whimsical interludes of delight rarely spotted in such utilitarian spaces—proof incarnate that some of the most exquisite things come in small packages.

CHAPTER OPENER: An atypical sink, cobalt-blue wallcovering, and a vintage mirror give this Chicago powder room by Alessandra Branca power. ABOVE: An atmospheric palette, along with a quiet botanical pattern, sets the scene in a storied Park Avenue apartment by Ashley Whittaker; the slick black lacquer grounds it all. OPPOSITE PAGE: A whimsical wallpaper with a mazelike parterre design energizes a powder room by Nick Olsen with dashing color and movement.

ABOVE: Romantic silk wallpaper creates a composed, calming effect in this Virginia home by Suzanne Kasler.
OPPOSITE PAGE: In an Upper East Side residence, Katie Ridder establishes a romantic sense of nostalgia with antique floral wallpaper; the suspended marble sink in a sharp profile prevents an overly sweet effect.

"Clients have things they have loved, collected, or purchased when they've traveled, and I always work with them on finding a place in their homes for that. It makes it more personal. A great interior is about a well-traveled eye and a sensibility that has depth and soul—not just one dimension."

—James Huniford

OPPOSITE PAGE: Antique silver paper puts a gleam on the walls of a
James Huniford–designed Nashville space.

ABOVE LEFT: The hand-painted blooms on the wall covering of this Anthony Baratta–designed space in Los Angeles bubble with joie de vivre or "joy of life." ABOVE RIGHT: Mirrored walls modernize, while copper sink fittings and a limestone vanity imbue the space with timelessness in this Atlanta home by architect D. Stanley Dixon. OPPOSITE PAGE: Custom-made mirrored surfaces in a Houston home by J. Randall Powers alchemize a glittering space.

ABOVE: A divided mirror lends architecture to a cozy Manhattan powder room, sheathed in an unexpected, playful pattern by Ashley Whittaker. OPPOSITE PAGE: Lacquered in plum, a Hamptons powder room by Luis Bustamante and architect Steven Harris becomes an unexpected thrill.

"To make your home feel more intimate, less is more—which is the reverse of what most people think. Large-scale lamps, accessories, and art (and more art!) quiet a space while creating great intimacy."

—Melanie Turner

OPPOSITE PAGE: A hand-painted mural on paper befits a 1934 Regency-style home in Atlanta's Buckhead district, designed by Melanie Turner.

Hallway Heaven

Corridors are every bit as important, decorating-wise, as any other room in the house—perhaps even more so. It's in traveling that you prepare yourself for arrival, and no one is partial to a second-class journey. You could create an al fresco feeling in a crowded city by lining one with botanical prints (page 154), upholster the doors themselves in emerald leather with nailhead trim for unexpected detail (page 154), or line a narrow passage in yellow-and-white striped wallcovering to draw the eyes up (page 155). Do whatever you can to keep bland at bay, and you'll find your experience within your home improves step by step.

ABOVE LEFT: Hand-hewn logs and antique accents create a timeless-yet-functional look in the mudroom of a Tennessee cabin by Tammy Connor. ABOVE RIGHT: In the entrance hall, Nick Olsen boldly painted walls and placed a mix of furnishings to set the tone for a Dutchess County, New York, country house with personality. OPPOSITE PAGE: Alessandra Branca selected circa 1930 sconces to pop against the high-gloss black walls of a Chicago townhome's hallway.

ABOVE LEFT: Upholstered doors by Miles Redd use nailhead trim to mimic architectural details. ABOVE RIGHT: Antique botanical prints give a graceful look to a Manhattan hallway by Cathy Kincaid. OPPOSITE PAGE: Striped butter-yellow walls and powder-blue window treatments dress up a hall in architect James Carter's Birmingham home, designed with Jane Hawkins Hoke, where paintings are hung salon-style.

BEGUILING

baths

The maxim "Form before function" may make a majority of engineers tremble with trepidation, but it's all but requisite in the bath—no matter how small the room's footprint. Even the least high-maintenance among us while away a multitude of our hours there, so shouldn't the room be as well designed as the typically more flamboyant dining room? Of course. Designers are transforming the most private of rooms into spaces worthy of Instagram, injecting them with timeless copper soaking tubs (page 167) or even Louis XVI consoles beneath the sink (page 157). Expand the space visually with tall, narrow mirrors (page 164), or make it charming as an Old Hollywood Spanish cottage by sheathing it in cinematic blue-and-white tile (page 166). Don't forget the uncontested trick to lifelong bathroom enamoration—a constant rotation of plush, perfectly laundered towels for the Relais & Châteaux treatment, sans room service.

CHAPTER OPENER: Francophile designer Tara Shaw outfitted her New Orleans bathroom with a Louis XVI console-turned-sink vanity; the 18th-century chair is Swedish. ABOVE: John Oetgen lined an Atlanta bathroom with Portoro Extra marble and other unexpected elements—a leather bench and an antique French mirror. OPPOSITE PAGE: Downtown views are the focal point in a Manhattan space designed by CetraRuddy Architecture, with a soaking tub to take them all in.

"It's completely me, and that's what you want your place to be—an extension of your inner self."

—Shawn Henderson

ABOVE: Tall mirrors create the illusion of a larger bathroom in a Manhattan apartment by Jeffrey Bilhuber. OPPOSITE PAGE: Fixtures with patina give the glass-walled bath by Steve and Brooke Giannetti in Ojai, California, a timeless grace.

ABOVE: A copper tub from London shines in the guesthouse bath of a North Shore, Long Island, home by Frank de Biasi. OPPOSITE PAGE: Blue-and-white Portuguese tiling in this bathroom designed by Mark D. Sikes makes it look more like Lisbon than Montecito.

"I like to be surrounded by objects that I have some kind of connection to. I'm a collector—the more the merrier! It makes things cozy for me. If I'm at an art fair, I always try to pick something up that I love—it doesn't have to be big; it's a memento of a trip and a time."

—Anthony Baratta

OPPOSITE PAGE: A quilt hung on the wall of an Anthony Baratta–designed Utah ski-lodge bathroom warms at a glance.

Marvelous Mirrors

If Lewis Carroll's 1871 novel *Through the Looking Glass* proved anything, it's that reality isn't always as it appears. In the design world, that translates to mirrors that transform spaces in acts of sheer wizardry. The reflective surface is veritable decorating magic: it can visually double a room, bounce light around, or, in the case of this Tuscany-inspired entry hall (left) by designer Laurie Steichen, create an orangerie for the ages—all within in an estimated 12 square feet. The antique mirror casts an otherworldly tenor over the room, expanding the lush and leafy greenery and announcing immediately that this is no cookie-cutter house. Cause for reflection, incarnate.

ABOVE: A rattan console by Betty Cobonpue and a travertine mirror turn this Nashville hallway designed by James Huniford into a house of haute art. OPPOSITE PAGE: In a California retreat by Laurie Steichen, an antique mirror and Venetian table turn a passageway into a beguiling destination all its own.

dining with
DISTINCTION

That tired, timeworn edict that you are what you eat applies equally to the dining room. The place of many dinner party amusements trumpets so much about who you are and what you love, be it your classical leanings, in a table ringed by antique Biedermeier chairs (page 179); your affection for the summer season, in a beachy blue and white space with rattan fittings (pages 190–191); or your not-so-secret desire to live out

174

Francophile fantasies in a Versailles-esque antiqued mirrored room (page 181). If your space has an abnormally small footprint, fear not: designers know how to play it with panache. Sheathe the walls in floral wallcovering for an al fresco feeling, even under the cloak of winter (page 186). Adding a photograph with extensive depth of field (page 176) can be a ruse, making a space appear more expansive than it is.

CHAPTER OPENER: A showstopping antique chandelier and custom mirror transform this Palm Beach breakfast nook by Markham Roberts into an early morning oasis. ABOVE: Ceilings are lacquered to appear higher, then framed with a newly designed classical molding, in this New York pied-à-terre by Cathy Kincaid. OPPOSITE PAGE: With space at a premium in this Park Avenue home by Celerie Kemble, the dining room doubles as a library; a photograph by Brian McKee visually expands the space with an optical illusion.

ABOVE: The antique Biedermeier chairs that ring this Manhattan table bestow a sense of timelessness, thanks to designer Tammy Connor. OPPOSITE PAGE: Black walls and a matching custom banquette allow an 18th-century Italian chandelier and 19th-century Italian farm table to take pride of place in the kitchen nook of this Atlanta townhouse by John Oetgen.

ABOVE: In this Upper East Side dining room, a quirky table, 18th-century Italian mirror, and vintage Mies van der Rohe chairs look ageless together, courtesy of designer Alecia Stevens and McBride Architects. OPPOSITE PAGE: A collection of art found mostly at Paris flea markets is hung over mirrored walls for visual interest in Mark D. Sikes's Hollywood Hills abode.

ABOVE: A whitewashed wooden ceiling lends rough-hewn softness to Colette van den Thillart's lakeside cabin, by architect Wayne Swadron, in the Ontario hinterlands. OPPOSITE PAGE: Mirrored walls and an expertly placed banquette expand the dining area of Thomas Hamel's Victorian-era Sydney apartment.

ABOVE: The striking near-black walls and ebonized floors in Susan Ferrier's Atlanta home supply a sense of intrigue.
OPPOSITE PAGE: In the octagonal dining room of the newly built Birmingham home of architect James Carter, built-in bookshelves and plainspoken bare floors lend rustic, historic charm to fine antique furnishings.

ABOVE: Colette van den Thillart's Toronto dining room evokes the feeling of a garden grotto, with an antique chandelier and a plaster wall piece that reads "Wilder Shores of Love." OPPOSITE PAGE: Vintage black leather chairs add high contrast and a modern twist to a Cathy Kincaid–designed Dallas dining room with an 18th-century Swedish chandelier and antique French table.

ABOVE: Custom cabinetry gives an antique-library look to a sitting area off the kitchen of a Malibu home by Martyn Lawrence Bullard. OPPOSITE PAGE: Miles Redd combines old and new in an informal Manhattan dining room, pairing Louis XV chairs with a Saarinen table. FOLLOWING PAGES: Woven hyacinth dining chairs, designed by Atlanta's Danielle Rollins, are a perfect complement to her breakfast room's vintage wicker chest and blue-and-white chinoiserie.

"People who love to read want their books to be out front and exposed. Then there are people who are obsessed with cleanliness and don't want clothes to touch each other in their closet. You have to understand what you appreciate most in life."

—John Saladino

OPPOSITE PAGE: The breakfast area of a New York apartment designed by John Saladino blends the ageless and contemporary in a multifunctional room.

192

ABOVE: Peter Dunham arranged a casual corner for dining in a Manhattan apartment, saving room with élan, thanks to a custom banquette; art by James Nares elevates the space. OPPOSITE PAGE: In winter, event designer Keith Robinson's Georgia dining table overflows with lush citrus and sweets.

Secret Collections

Displaying your cache is like opening a bay window to your soul—and keeping it curated is requisite to veil any hoarding tendencies. Designers are almost always furtive hoarders; most of them will even admit to it (and their stockpiled storage units). So look to the professionals for clever solutions for arranging finds in decorative—not off-putting—ways. You could, if the object in question suits, hang it overhead—as Charlotte Moss did with her beloved garden baskets in her East Hampton potting shed (page 201). Or arrange your posy of floral china as blooms bursting forth from a curio cabinet (page 200), with the cabinet in question summoning a florist's store-front. It's all about working with what the gods of collecting gave you—and doing them proud. Keeping finds tucked behind the cloak of a closet door won't do it.

ABOVE: A collection of monotone vintage watering cans and flowerpots decorates the chicken coop of Steve and Brooke Giannetti's Ojai property. OPPOSITE PAGE: Displaying collections in a unified color palette is more cohesive—making them curated, not cluttered.

ABOVE: Painted African baskets and a collection of vintage whisk brooms adorn Richard Hallberg's Montecito dining room. OPPOSITE PAGE: A pantry's glass door puts a tidy collection of fine china on exhibition in a 1930s Dallas colonial designed by Cathy Kincaid.

ABOVE: Display collections of like-colored china—such as this garden-inspired trove—in a fitting curio cabinet that strikes the same note. OPPOSITE PAGE: A hoard of garden baskets becomes functional art in Charlotte Moss's East Hampton potting shed.

ABOVE: A few accumulated treasures of London-based designer Alidad pop against his buttercup-yellow walls. OPPOSITE PAGE: In a historic Dallas home, Cathy Kincaid displays the owner's collection of blue-and-white porcelain inspired by the dining room's palette.

MAXIMIZED
kitchens

Before kitchens became founts of tech-forward wizardry, where garden asparagus can be steamed Kelly green in mere seconds and dishes wash themselves at the push of a button, they contained one life-sustaining appliance: the hearth. The reasons your brunch guests buzz around countertop crudités and charcuterie can trace their roots to that one, exceedingly primal raison d'être. It's fitting, then, that kitchens are habitually the sites of overblown remodeling budgets—it's because they truly matter, and they're worth it. Alchemize them into the flickering flames they are by imbuing them with over-the-top hallmarks of your personal taste, be that painting the cabinets a high-gloss eggplant hue, the same shade as your favorite bird (page 222), or hiring an artist to whimsically apply your Delftware patterns writ large upon the walls themselves (page 209). Even if all you ever do there is pop open bottles and plate delivery, it will be a personal haven that speaks to you— and seems to listen, too.

CHAPTER OPENER: Cerused-oak cabinetry and chevron wood flooring balance stainless steel appliances and surfaces in this Windy City kitchen by Alessandra Branca. ABOVE: Painted walls mimic Delft pottery with a larger-than-life scale in a characterful Long Island, New York, kitchen by Thomas Britt. OPPOSITE PAGE: Soaring exposed-beam ceilings in the same color palette as the walls lend this John Oetgen–designed hideaway in North Carolina a palatial air. FOLLOWING PAGES: Shelves make the log walls of this Tennessee cabin by Tammy Connor look lighter than they are.

ABOVE: Traditional touches imbue a new high-rise kitchen 30 floors above Houston with a sense of permanence. OPPOSITE PAGE: Buttoned-up preppy touches, like Parisian bistro chairs and stripes at every turn, balance a mod Saarinen table in this Newport home by Ruthie Sommers.

FACING PAGE: A trip to Denmark inspired Colette van den Thillart's Ontario kitchen—especially the island's marbleized design.

214

ABOVE: In a Matthew Quinn kitchen in Nashville, suspended shelves increase countertop space.
OPPOSITE PAGE: Sparked by the style of the late Bunny Mellon, Nick Olsen had the kitchen floor of a Dutchess County, New York, home painted in an eye-popping graphic pattern.

FACING PAGES:
Functionality is key in
this New York kitchen by
Katie Leede, where the
island is used for dining
and perfecting work
presentations—and as a
bar for cocktail parties.

ABOVE: Kathryn M. Ireland's Venice, California, kitchen balances new (cement countertops) with old (vintage pendants).
OPPOSITE PAGE: Pale woods and creamy whites brighten Suzanne Tucker and Timothy Marks's small, sunny Montecito bungalow.

ABOVE: Cabinet backs are covered in patterned fabric that provides a traditional foil to the disco ball overhead, adding shimmer to walls and millwork in a kitchen designed by Ashley Whittaker. OPPOSITE PAGE: Limestone walls inspired the creamy tones of the furnishings in Marston Luce's breakfast nook, with its vintage coffee table and a 19th-century French lantern. FOLLOWING PAGES: A floor of chestnut planks reclaimed from a Tennessee barn and a large hearth give a new Long Island kitchen by Frank de Biasi and architect Leonard Woods a classic look.

ABOVE: Graphic prints and geometric floors energize the service area of Danielle Rollins's Atlanta kitchen. OPPOSITE PAGE: Peter Dunham designed this industrial kitchen island in Manhattan to double as an impromptu dining space.

gardens with
GRANDEUR

One doesn't have to own an estate on par with Edith Wharton's The Mount to purloin her exact plantings—white begonia and linden trees, dahlias and delphinium. After all, the most alluring charms of a garden are the size of a David Austin rosebud, or flitting butterflies on the lam. Nurture the same plants you've taken note of on your travels, if your particular longitude can nourish them, so that even your grounds burst with personal memory, leaf by verdant leaf. When laying out your exterior decor, treat it like any other much-adored room in your house—albeit in weather-ready materials and outdoor fabrics. Designers imbue even postage-stamp-size garden plots with grandeur and tend blossoming ideas you might take as cues in your own yard, such as allowing grasses to grow wild and deliciously feral along a tidy path for contrast (page 237), or manicuring hedges as carefully as Kate Middleton tends her coiffure (page 249). Bend your garden to your interests, perhaps by planting a row of arbors with sinuous climbing vines over an al fresco dining table (pages 260–261), or even pressing shells into a cement wall in an epitome of folk-art shell craft (page 238). Garden variety it's not.

CHAPTER OPENER: Taupe-colored lounge chairs face a fire pit and built-in seating designed by Scott Shrader, with cushions and throw pillows in a variety of muted hues. ABOVE: Set under an old oak tree atop pebbled grounds, an al fresco dining table at the Ojai home of Steve and Brooke Giannetti—complete with an antique farm table—feels as far-flung as a Provençal summer. OPPOSITE PAGE: Placing a lone sculptural bench—such as this antique faux bois one—in a clean-lined outdoor space like this one by garden designer Hilary Finn can make it read larger; the white pebbled floor adds a sense of luminousness.

ABOVE: Blue-and-white textures temper a riot of foliage on this outdoor terrace in Paris. OPPOSITE PAGE: A hammock like this one, at the East Hampton home of Charlotte Moss, with all the comforts of home—a blanket, a book, and a place to rest your bubbly—ensures you'll actually use it.

ABOVE: The entry courtyard of a Dallas home by Emily Summers and architect Marc Appleton becomes a transportive al fresco getaway, thanks to symmetrically placed carved stone benches. OPPOSITE PAGE: A garden path is surrounded by native grasses and river birch in this Hamptons home with landscaping by David Kelly.

ABOVE: A tufa-stone fountain in the Italian garden of a Hamptons home incorporates oak benches for reflection below an arbor of espaliered pear trees and elaborate yew hedges. OPPOSITE PAGE: Sculptor Simon Verity and architect Martha Finney fashioned a fanciful grotto from tufa stone, seashells, and quartz.

ABOVE: Urns purchased at auction make a Hamptons butterfly-patterned gate, shrouded in honeysuckle and Félicité Parmentier roses, even more stately. OPPOSITE PAGE: A screened outdoor play area in Colette van den Thillart's Ontario summer cabin becomes the ultimate napping nook with its antique bed. FOLLOWING PAGES: A Ming dynasty dog statue arises from a cluster of boxwoods in this Connecticut garden by landscape architect Charles Stick.

ABOVE: A fanciful Chinese pavilion, topped with a gilded pineapple, occupies an island within the Connecticut estate gardens by landscape artist Charles Stick. The perfect spot for tea in the late afternoon, the pavilion is accessible by stepping-stones over the koi pond. OPPOSITE PAGE: Painted in pale blue, the ceiling of a Nick Olsen–decorated clapboard house, built in 1747 in Dutchess County, New York, becomes an ever-present sunny sky to lounge under.

ABOVE: Mary McDonald's outdoor loggia takes indoor-outdoor living to new heights, with lush stripes and checks, painted Gustavian chairs, and even a Chippendale-style gilt mirror. OPPOSITE PAGE: Rustic twig furniture rings a tulip table for an al fresco Nick Olsen dining space that won't tire.

ABOVE: Rattan pendant lights echo the rattan chairs in Kathryn M. Ireland's Venice, California, outdoor dining area. OPPOSITE PAGE: A carved 18th-century urn looks as fitting on a small terrace as it does within the manicured hedges of John Saladino's Montecito property. FOLLOWING PAGES: The lush grounds of a home designed by Frank de Biasi and architect Leonard Woods, with landscape design by Innocenti & Webel, on Long Island's North Shore include an orchid greenhouse inspired by the structures of Colonial Williamsburg.

ABOVE: Symmetry rules on John Saladino's Montecito terrace, where weathered wood furniture emits a fuss-free vibe. OPPOSITE PAGE: A vase brimming with Viburnum opulus takes center stage in Keith Robinson's Georgia garden-party tablescape.

ABOVE: Surrounded by boxwood, European wild ginger, and impatiens, a medieval pigeonnier, or dovecote, still stands in the garden of Marston Luce's French farmhouse. OPPOSITE PAGE: Arches of espaliered apple trees frame event designer Keith Robinson's Georgia table, set along a path bordered by tomato beds.

ABOVE: Tucking a custom banquette against the walls allows the fire pit of this Ojai home some protection from summer breezes. OPPOSITE PAGE: Seasonal flowers in vintage vases form a fitting centerpiece for a countryside garden party.

ABOVE: In tailored blue and white that balances the frenetic city below, Michael S. Smith's Manhattan terrace is an ideal perch for a breezy get-together. OPPOSITE PAGE: Bistro chairs complement a casual-chic vibe in an outdoor dinner party by Laura Vinroot Poole. Colorful birdcages in all shapes and sizes house votive candles that will offer light when the sun goes down. FOLLOWING PAGES: *Jasminum tortuosum* adds an additional note of fragrance under a Montecito rose arbor of homeowner Oprah Winfrey.

ABOVE: In Colette van den Thillart's Toronto home, the garden is a welcome respite on warm days. OPPOSITE PAGE: Keith Robinson selected moody cranberry and blue linens to contrast with the surrounding foliage for his Georgia dinner party.

264

Grow Green

Maidenhair fern, string-of-pearls, widow's-thrill: plant names are evocative because plants themselves are evocative. Their organic dispositions confer literal life into any interior and draw the eye like light itself. Place a small potted darling in an otherwise dull corner for an injection of vivacity (left), or use a skyscraping palm to accentuate a tall space (above). If you sing or whisper compliments to them as you water, you'll find yourself growing like a spring sprout with each sighting of a plucky new leaf.

ABOVE: Framed prints draw the eye up in a diminutive study in Jan Showers's Dallas home. OPPOSITE PAGE: An antiqued mirror reflects a candelabra-inspired fixture in this Montecito space by Mark D. Sikes.

Photography Credits

© **Melanie Acevedo:** 11, 218, interior design by Katie Leede, produced by Carolyn Englefield; 26, interior design by Charlotte Moss, architecture by Dale Bocher, landscape design by Lisa Stamm, produced by Carolyn Englefield; 28, 68, 101, 106, interior design by Andrew Brown, produced by Carolyn Englefield; 39, 118, 189, interior design by Miles Redd, architecture by Thomas Vail, produced by Carolyn Englefield; 41, 42, 89, architectural, interior, and landscape design by Cheryl Skoog Tague, produced by Carolyn Englefield; 124, interior design by Ann Getty & Associates, produced by Carolyn Englefield; 190, 226, interior design by Danielle Rollins, architecture by Bill Ingram, landscape design by John Howard, produced by Carolyn Englefield; 201, 234, interior design by Charlotte Moss, architecture by Dale Bocher, landscape design by Lisa Stamm, produced by Carolyn Englefield; 258, produced by Catherine Lee Davis

© **Mali Azima:** 53, 129, 130, 151, interior design by Melanie Turner, architecture by Pak Heyot & Associates, landscape design by Land Plus Associates; 216, interior design by Michael Quinn, styled by Eleanor Roper

© **Quentin Bacon:** 38

© **Alexandre Bailhache:** 116, 117, 223, 254, interior design by Marston Luce, produced by Carolyn Englefield

© **Sylvie Becquet:** 235, produced by Catherine Lee Davis

© **Tim Beddow:** 2, 50

© **Bruce Buck/The New York Times/ Redux:** 161

Pamela Cook/Studio D: 198

© **Roger Davies:** 27, 146 left, interior design by Anthony Baratta, architecture by Steve Giannetti, landscape architecture by Perry Guillot; 32, 81, 220, interior design by Suzanne Tucker and Timothy Marks, produced by Carolyn Englefield; 34, 66, interior and landscape design by Mark D. Sikes, produced by Carolyn Englefield; 90, interior design by Martyn Lawrence Bullard, architecture by Doug Burdge, landscape design by James Hyatt, produced by Carolyn Englefield

© **Erica George Dines:** 17, 18, 23, 153 left, 210 interior design by Tammy Connor, architecture by James Carter, styled by Thea Beasley; 8, 94, 184, interior design by Susan Ferrier, architecture by Jonathan Torode

© **Chris Edwards for More:** 259

© **Miguel Flores-Vianna:** 193

© **Tria Giovan:** 212, 238, 239, 240, back cover

© **Max Kim-Bee:** cover, 74, interior design by Robert Couturier, produced by Carolyn Englefield; 14, interior design by Richard Hallberg, architecture by Appleton & Associates, landscape design by Clark and White; 44, 195, 227, interior design by Peter Dunham, architecture

by Andrew Franz Architect, produced by Carolyn Englefield; 63, interior design by Kelli Ford and Kirsten Fitzgibbons; 83, 84, 88, 108, 186, 262, interior design by Colette Van Den Thillart, produced by Carolyn Englefield; 92, 170, interior design by Laurie Steichen, architecture by M. Carbine Restorations, produced by Carolyn Englefield; 103, interior design by Tim Howard, produced by Carolyn Englefield; 113, 149, 222, interior design by Ashley Whittaker, architecture by Jim Joseph, produced by Carolyn Englefield; 121, 167, 224, 250, interior design by Frank de Biasi, architecture by Leonard Woods, landscape design by Innocenti & Webel, produced by Carolyn Englefield; 123, 208, interior design by John Oetgen, produced by Carolyn Englefield; 144, 171, interior design by James Huniford; 148, 237, interior design by Luis Bustamante, architecture by Steven Harris, landscape design by David Kelly, produced by Pilar Crespi; 157, interior design by Tara Shaw, architecture by Barry Fox, landscape design by Byron Adams and Wanda Metz Chase, produced by Carolyn Englefield; 166, 264, interior design by Mark D. Sikes, produced by Carolyn Englefield; 183, 214, 241, 133 left, interior design by Colette Van Den Thillart, architecture by Wayne S. Wadron, landscape design by Blackrock Landscapes, produced by Carolyn Englefield; 199, interior design and landscape design by Richard Hallberg, produced by Carolyn Englefield; 209, interior design by Thomas Britt; 242, 244, landscape architecture by Charles Stick, produced by Carolyn Englefield

Index

HEARSTBOOKS

An Imprint of Sterling Publishing Co., Inc.
1166 Avenue of the Americas
New York, NY 10036

ISBN 978-1-61837-284-0

Distributed in Canada by Sterling Publishing Co., Inc.
c/o Canadian Manda Group, 664 Annette Street
Toronto, Ontario M6S 2C8, Canada
Distributed in the United Kingdom by GMC Distribution Services
Castle Place, 166 High Street, Lewes, East Sussex BN7 1XU, England
Distributed in Australia by NewSouth Books
University of New South Wales, Sydney, NSW 2052, Australia

For information about custom editions, special sales, and premium and corporate purchases,
please contact Sterling Special Sales at 800-805-5489 or specialsales@sterlingpublishing.com.

Manufactured in China

2 4 6 8 10 9 7 5 3 1

sterlingpublishing.com
veranda.com

Cover design by Elizabeth Mihaltse Lindy
Interior design by Think Studio
Photography credits on page 266